the eaters of flowers

the eaters of flowers

poems

ire'ne lara silva

SADDLE ROAD PRESS

Saddle Road Press
Ithaca, New York
saddleroadpress.com

ISBN 9798987954126
Library of Congress Control Number: 2023939721

Cover art "puño de flores" by Octavio Quintanilla
octavioquintanilla.com
Cover and book design by Don Mitchell

Books by ire'ne lara silva
furia
Blood Sugar Canto
CUICACALLI/House of Song
FirstPoems
Enduring Azucares
Hibiscus Tacos
flesh to bone

Contents

hibiscus

in my heart	11
the story of my four hearts	12
i know they mean well when they say	
my brother is still with me	13
it's the old hunger to grow wild	14
i have more freedom now	15
she said she didn't know how to make medicine	16
Lot K32	17

dandelion

taking inventory	21
i see no reason	24
mala hierba	26
puño de flores	27
mo(u)rning song	28
navigating grief	29
silence is the breath between songs	31

rose

there is some consolation in black asphalt	35
poem for my kidneys	36
the blank canvas	38
what the curandera said	40
we say *rose*	41
the sound of rain	42
what the hospice nurse asked	43
the eaters of flowers	45

marigold

descanso   51
the pain of the body is sacred   52
my mother would say   54
alone   57
it's been 6 months   59
cempasuchil   60
what my brother said   62
gracias a mis diosas   64

the last poem

about the last poem   66
for Uvalde   67

Acknowledgments   69
About ire'ne lara silva   71

dedicated to my brother and adopted son
Moisés Salvador Luciano Lara
11/02/1981 – 07/24/2022
mi Xochipilli

and with gratitude pa' mis diosas
La Guadalupe, Coatlicue, y Mi Niña Blanca

hibiscus

in my heart

in my heart no circus
in my heart no cages
in my heart no stampedes
in my heart no whirlpools
in my heart no quicksand
in my heart no raging fires
in my heart no guilt
in my heart no shame
in my heart no chaos
in my heart no bitterness
in my heart nothing left unsaid

in my heart tawny fields of tall grass
in my heart drifting clouds
in my heart flowering vines
in my heart mesquites and huizaches
in my heart sycamores and cedars
in my heart every small and humble green
in my heart blooming ocotillos and crowns of thorns
in my heart the peaceful lapping of the wide river
in my heart the light of his eyes that will never leave me
in my heart a thousand thousand conversations
in my heart the hand i held even after it went cold

my friend said: you see, hardly anyone knows what peaceful grief looks like

the story of my four hearts

the first one i pulled out of my chest at twenty-three
tangled roots trailing earth everywhere
it wouldn't stop loving
and i needed it to stop loving

the second died of atrophy
withered with loss after loss
bruised with work and pain and worry
i didn't even feel when it stopped beating

the third was a surprise and a gift
a flowering fruited thing
that kept offering itself everywhere
will you love me? will you love me?

the third heart died with my brother
it exploded from grief
and left me lost
in a crater of howling emptiness

at four months this fourth heart
is now old enough
to tell me its name
it is my cast iron heart

i grew it slowly and deliberately
not knowing if it'd be my last heart
made of iron and steel melted at 2800 degrees
all the impurities burned out

tempered with time
tempered with intention
my cast iron heart doesn't ask
to be loved it just loves

all my hearts were born writing
i'm listening for what the cast iron one will say

i know they mean well when they say my brother is still with me

i know they mean well when they say my brother is still with me
but i hope he isn't in his last days he was forgetting where he was
and my name and his own name he was forgetting all of it and he
knew only enough to trust my voice and my hand holding his hand
and that he wasn't alone and that i would take care of anything he
needed i hope he's walked on to the next world without any
memory of this one hope he's forgotten all the pain all the anger i
hope he's forgotten his childhood and my father forgotten bullies
and homophobes forgotten bruises and broken hearts forgotten
despair and hurt i hope he's forgotten doctors and painkillers and
surgeries and hospitals and wounds and pain oh i hope i hope he's
forgotten pain

                even if it means he's forgotten me even if our
difficult years and our beautiful years live only in my heart even if
he doesn't remember all our adventures all our tears all our laughter
even if he doesn't remember our years of colors and words and
music and flowers because even when he didn't know my name he
still smiled at me and looked so kindly upon me and i couldn't have
prayed for anything more at his peaceful moment of passing i hope
he remembers nothing even if it means i send all this love that still
lives in me out in no particular direction

                      in the first rain afterwards
i saw him in the white rain lilies sprouting roadside saw him in the
greening of the revived blades of grass saw him when the leaves
started to change color and i saw him when the crimson crown of
thorns started blooming may his spirit be racing in delight from one
streak of lightning to another may it be curled in comfort in the
petals of roses and peonies may it be watching in wide eyed delight
as the dew forms each morning may his spirit be drifting in the soft
clouds overhead may it be visiting the snow covered chollas
blooming a soft yellow may his spirit be running with the howling
of the coyotes i heard tonight and last night and the night before

it's the old hunger to grow wild

and sprout poems
to make composted earth of my flesh and my breath   earth turned
relentlessly   and simmered slowly with the weight of memory and
desire and the deep deep clench of muscle and yearning

i ate the seeds   i ate all the seeds   bit them   chewed
them let them rest on my tongue   tasted their sweet their bitter their
salt   i gathered the roots gossamer and rough knotted things and
branching masses in my hands and shoved them into my hair

the earth must think us flowers   flowers of meat and
air flowers that grunt and weep and laugh   slow flowers that uncurl
and reach for the sun and bloom and seed and darken and wither and
fall   flowers that crumble like all flowers that will feed her

i will give you more flowers than you can eat   push
them into your mouth with my mouth   lick them into you   thrust
them into the hollow of your chest   curl them beneath your eyelids
whisper them over your skin until they dissolve into you

i am eating flowers and the petals are spilling out of
my mouth out of my eyes   out of me spilling and spilling   i am
birthing flowers   devouring   devoured   blooming bursting i am
eating flowers   life eating life   death eating   death   my   flesh
flowers

i have more freedom now

he asked
does it always come with loss?

        and i said yes
though i didn't know that before

i never counted
the cost when i was younger

        childhood left me
feral and willing to gnaw

in my youth
freedom was worth any-/every-thing

        and as life became
a series of cages—jobs bills doctors

i turned inwards
and sought my freedoms there

        approaching fifty
i have accumulated losses

upon losses
unwieldy burdens often jostled

        barely held in the now
impossible expanse of my arms

and this freedom now
this greatest freedom i have ever lived

        is paid the cost being the
only price i never would have chosen to pay

she said she didn't know how to make medicine

but i do   i know how to make medicine what else
was i given life for   i have been watching and
learning whispering and praying   breathing and
weeping   living and living and living

and breaking my skin and breaking my eyes and
breaking my heart and breaking my thoughts
grinding down the fragments in a molcajete made of
what survives when a star explodes

so many drops of my blood in this   so many drops
of my bile   so many drops of my tears this is what
no one tells you   that there is medicine you can
make of yourself   no green leaves no blossoms

we are in the place where there are no recipes no
instructions   but   where you must walk gently on
the earth and clear your eyes and do no harm and
break none of the laws of medicine

do you see   it's taken everything everything i am
and every second of what i've lived to even begin to
learn   my heart has died and my heart has died and
my heart has died and i keep breathing

medicine lives under my skin and in my eyes and in
my tongue and in my breath   i know how to make
medicine i speak medicine i walk medicine i am
becoming i am making myself medicine

Lot K32

it's roughly 3 feet by 7 feet
there are no lines to separate
one lot from another

wild grass wildflowers
a few small stones
spillover of red brown mulch
from the lot next to it

it's quiet here
the traffic is a far off sound
even though the road isn't far
it's all the trees mostly oaks
pecans cottonwoods cedars

it doesn't seem to matter
what time of the year it is
there are always butterflies
birds darting from place to place
green leaves on the trees
and golden leaves fluttering down

my brother is buried in Lot K31
we bought both plots at the same time
i didn't know his would be vacant
for such a very short time
i wonder if he knew different
wonder if he held on to make sure
i had a signed contract in hand

he was buried the way he wanted
on a wooden pallet
wrapped in a cotton shroud
surrounded with flowers
from head to foot
a bouquet laid over his chest
no coffin no concrete no embalming
no separation from the earth

before the year is out
it'll be five months since he was buried
i don't think it's my imagination
but the burial mound seems to be
as high as it ever was
the only thing that's different
is the permanent flat stone
that bears his name
and the dates of his life
and my name for him

when i visit i take
a little stepladder to sit on
i unfold it over Lot K32
because it seems disrespectful
to sit elsewhere and possibly
intrude on someone else's grave
at least here i know it's vacant
and i hope to leave it vacant
for at least another three decades
letting the leaves flutter down
and the wild grass grow

i took care of him
for all but seven years of his life
in the afterlife there will be
no need to look after each other
his spirit in the unfurling
of all green things and the dew
is free of all pain and memory
and mine will return to the wind
as free as it ever dreamed of being
but here beneath this earth
we will never leave each other
we will be siblings of the soil

dandelion

taking inventory

47 year old Hispanic female
    (not the label i'd use but you know how those forms are)
    (48 will be here before i know it. and then 50.
    i'm throwing the biggest party of my life for my 50th.
    i started planning it two years ago.
    i might cry all day because i'll be wearing the tiara
    my brother bought me right away. as if he knew
    he wouldn't live to see me turn 50.)

morbidly obese, diabetes, hypertension, hyperlipidimia
    (i think my bones alone weigh more than what that chart
    says i should weigh)
    (insulin dependent since April 23, 2008)
    (high blood pressure since i was a teen.
    it briefly went away after i left home at 18
    but came back every time family was near)
    (high cholesterol came with the diabetes)
    (of course, if you'd looked at my family
    medical history, all of these could have
    been predicted. might as well have been
    on the hospital bracelet i wore when i was born)

no surgeries, one hospitalization 2022
    (no broken bones. only one in my family who still
    has a gall bladder. i was 47 before i was ever in a
    hospital as a patient. two days after my brother
    passed—i think i short-circuited—between
    the broken heart and my body realizing it could
    finally rest. i spent three days in a beige room. My
    life had never been such a blank page.)

single, never married, no children.
    (i tell two stories about being single. the first is that
    my oldest sister, 17 years older than me, was cruel
    when she turned down her first marriage proposal.
    my mother said it was because he was too poor and
    dark-skinned. a tarot card reader told my sister that
    because of that she was destined to be the last daughter

to marry. in horror, she said that that couldn't possibly
also include toddler aged me. but here we are, i've
never married and neither has she.)
(at 24, i decided i wasn't going to have children. i had
four reasons. i only remember 2—i didn't want to
pass down my family's medical/psychological history
and i had no faith in the future of the world.)
(no children of my body. i adopted my brother in 2017
after his amputation so that i could keep my job and
take care of him. yes, FMLA.)

employed full-time
(they never give enough room on these forms to explain
fully. it seems like it should be important to explain
fully somewhere. i was put to work before i knew how
to spell my name. quite sure my parents had me so i could
work. the last time i tried to list everything i'd had 33 jobs.
that was more than 10 years ago. even now, counting down
to retirement and with only myself to take care of, i think
most people would count me as working 3 jobs. or 1 job
and a full blown career.)

high school education, some college
(my some college was Ivy League, but i don't think that counts
since i don't have that final piece of paper. hell if i'm ever going
back to school. for decades, there wasn't enough money or
time. i paid and paid the price of that with jobs that never paid
enough, but i built my writer life anyway. whether i live 5 years
or 50, i'm going to spend them all writing.)

question 1: do you have any dreams left?
i have more dreams than i know how to speak and i can
speak for hours. a peaceful home, simple and beautiful.
i want to sleep and daydream and read and think and take
all my time. i want to sing and laugh and grow strong
again and dance again. i want to fly here and there and
there and here. a hundred road trips. i want to spend
entire nights looking at the stars. i want to write books
and books and books. i want to talk to friends and share
meals and see new places and visit old places and

explore everything. i want to sit alone and i want to sit in company. i want to feel the wind and know that even though my freedom is born of grief and shaped with sorrow, it's still beautiful and it's still mine.

question 2: is this a poem or a rant?
        this is a poem.
        because i say it is.

i see no reason

to wait till the day of the dead
last time i left snickerdoodles
a little sweet stack of three
that had been delivered warm

tomorrow i'll take some of this
delicious posole with hominy
and blue corn and chile and
chicken and lime and cilantro

next time i might pick up the
fried mushrooms he loved
so much and cut them in half
and drizzle them with ranch

i ate the most beautiful thing
two months after he passed
i spent an afternoon with friends
making hibiscus tacos

on tiny yellow corn torillas
with queso fresco and pico
i cried and cried when i got
home, utterly inconsolable

because he'd never taste it
i'd never make them for him
never wait in delight for his
reaction or his request for more

i always loved that about him
how he delighted the way
i delighted in new flavors
and textures and spices

he would have loved that
i made them by instinct
without following a recipe
i followed my tastebuds

he would have loved
the deep purple and the
bright colors of the pico
de gallo and the white cheese

he would have loved
the poetry of eating flowers
not as decoration or afterthought
but as sustenance and intention

he would have loved
the poetry of eating flowers
as our ancestors ate them
savored and transformed

mala hierba

i like the idea of people yelling *nunca muere* at me on the
street at the store at the bar in the restaurant at the café at
the airport in the classroom at a reading while i'm talking
to friends or eating tacos or walking from one place to
another
      i imagine i won't need to do much more than flash
a quick smile and perhaps raise my hand in recognition
unless they yell *mala hierba* in which case i'll be the one
yelling *nunca muere* at them and then laughing with my
eyes burning bright
        i promised myself this tattoo after surviving
covid in 2020 before vaccines or boosters when the streets
were still empty and everything was closed and very few
people would talk about how many people were dying and
dying and dying
        i felt Death sitting by my bed filling
out my application for the Afterworld but fortunately it
was rejected and i cried the first day i was able to take a
shower and change my bedsheets stained with thirteen
days of blood, mucus, urine, and vomit
        there was a news story
about a Latino, my same age and from the Rio Grande
Valley who died of covid he'd left a beautiful letter for his
wife that the newspaper published and it was read on the
news and that letter made everyone cry
      but i read the
story and he got sick a day after i did and the day i cried
with relief he went to the hospital and the day i returned
to work was the day he died and i thought but for the grace
of god go i —
      i have always loved the wild strength of weeds
growing wherever they chose years ago i saw a dandelion
growing in a rain gutter the stalk tall and thick and it
seemed to be drinking in the moonlight *mala hierba* inked
on my skin and that dandelion in my mind's eye

puño de flores
after the frontexto by Octavio Quintanilla

one of my favorite Ramon Ayala songs says
that all you'll take with you is a fistful of earth

i think if death is a fistful of earth
then life must be a fistful of flowers

held loose held fiercely held carelessly
held as if our skin could taste their colors

as if we could drink in the sunshine they fed on
as if we could catch the scent of the rain they drank

as if the stems were made of light not earth
as if the stems spoke in electricity and sang in sinew

as if each flower was someone we'd loved as much
or more than we'd loved ourselves—for a time at least

as if each crease or dark edge on a petal was a pain
we'd endured and taken so deep it had renamed us

held as if we could convince them to endure forever
even as the heat of our hands shortened their time

mo(u)rning song

when all the things in me
that are sad and bleeding
grow quiet and still

i will think of the wild
morning glory that grew
in my mother's garden

in inhospitable soil
under a too bright sun
and never enough moisture

like no other morning
glory i ever saw its green
a pale green its petals silver

full and glorious in the dew
of the soft soft morning
as if it had never been hidden

as if its destiny of a few short
hours wasn't already written
a destiny clenched and wrinkled

because it was already dreaming
of the morning to come and all
the mornings that would follow

no not dreaming not wishing
not even praying it knows it
knows it will be glorious again

as hard as the earth may be
as much as the sun might hurt
as much as its roots might thirst

i'll never stop mourning but i'll
never not think too of my mother's
morning glory blooming silver

navigating grief

i've never been overwhelmed by choices
i can choose things all day—what to do
where to go what to say what to work on
who to be with what i want for my life
what i'll wear where i'll drive what errand
is most important what bill to pay what today's
priority is and tomorrow's and the day after's
where i'll be buried and whether or not i want
to say yes and what book i'll read next and
what i want to eat and whether or not i want
to see the sun rise or the sun set or the clouds
hurtling purple across the night sky

when my choices were limited i said if i can't
do what i want i'll do what i can and i kept on
choosing and choosing and never looked back

i just told a lie i lied when i said i'd never
been overwhelmed by choices it happened
only one time in my life right after my brother
died and after twenty years of choosing one
thing after another together and after twenty
years of compromising and twenty years of
choosing for us i found myself alone and
didn't know what was most important anymore
and didn't know when to eat or when to sleep
and it seemed infinite this work of choosing
what to do for myself minute after minute
after minute hour after hour day after day
realizing that my choices were proliferating
by the minute

i linger now wait to see if i will need to change
my mind mostly i linger now to see which
choice will hurt more and if the hurt is too much

do i choose to stay in the city of memories do
i create a life in a city he never knew do i
choose to stay in the home of memories in the
home where we spent our happiest years and
where he took his last breaths do i eat this
favorite meal of ours alone or do i wait another
month or two or twelve do i watch this favorite
movie of ours alone or do i wait or will waiting
mean nothing and the memories will stab me
again as sharply and i'll lose him all over again
and are the memories and the hurt a comfort to
convince me that it was all real that i didn't
imagine all of those years and in the end is it
the city that is populated with memories or is it
all after all only me

a tumult of pain and memories and love and
grief all tumbled and tossed and ricocheting inside
one person as i feel out which direction to take next

silence is the breath between songs

singing is inviting all the ghosts all of my dead to sing and in my voice
their voice and in my voice all the songs i have loved and all the times
my heart thrilled and sank and soared and in my voice all the voices
that have or ever will sing with me in the singing all my lost loves all
my broken hearts all the far flung shattered pieces of my soul all the
sharp edges lined in red all the times i wept and all the times i laughed
and all the times i prayed and all the times i gave thanks in the singing
everything i have ever held precious and all the times i fought and
everything i kept quiet and everything i didn't and in the singing never
one voice in the singing all the voices i have ever sung with all the
voices that have sung with me and in the singing there is no time no
differentiation of then or now or future no differentiation of here or
there or living or dead in the singing neither love nor heartbreak ever
forget themselves and a single phrase lingers through decades never
diminishing in the singing voices that braid themselves through a life
and i will hear singing on my last day even if i am silent

rose

there is some consolation in black asphalt

that can't be found anywhere else something in the stretch of the road
the way it rolls the way the tires rumble over it that unknots unspools
your flesh something in the roar of the open windows in the loud, loud
music and the voices soaring over all of it

there is some consolation that can't be found anywhere else not in
conversation with friends not in drink or distraction or sleep or in
the arms of strangers or not-strangers not in creating or reading or
cleaning or running or praying

unless this is a form of prayer watching the night sky that isn't as dark
as the trees the trees impenetrably dense the trees that are still the
trees that move in the wind the trees that smell sweet now that winter
is here the trees that leaf and die leaf and die

and the headlights never waiver as cars pass ahead or fall behind
as traffic thickens and thins and every sign is reassuring every familiar
sign and every sign never noticed before it's reassuring that the road is
wide and mostly smooth

and the road never ends and the road never says not now and the
 road knows the light of the sun even at night and whether it's day
or night the road reaches to touch the sky at every point and
sometimes we forget we are roads we are made of roads

poem for my kidneys

this starts as a poem for my kidneys but as you'll see it will rapidly
become a poem about mortality maybe really everything is about mortality
because i'm not sure we can really be serious about anything unless death
is part of the equation whether the subject is war or pandemic or famine or
violence or oppression or history or the environment

                                        do we really even
know what prayer is unless death has bitten at our heels or taken someone
we loved or threatened to   before that moment prayer might just be *i want
i want i want*   though perhaps a kind family may have taught prayer to be
all *thank you thank you thank you*   though i might still ask if we know
how to be grateful before we've lost anything

                                        as i was saying this is a poem
for my kidneys my kidneys that don't need a specialist   yet
said the doctor   not yet   but i've been on insulin for almost
fifteen years and the labs have always said too much protein is getting
through and my doctor gave me the vaccine for hepatitis b years ago the
entire course because infections from dialysis are rampant

                                        we never discuss
it in company   how we might die only how we'd like to die
peacefully in our sleep and in old age and surrounded by loved ones we
say although an adventurous   few might say   in a sudden and fiery
explosion gone just like that all at once no one says alone in a hospital no
one says in excruciating pain no one says after a long illness

                                        my father's
people died of cancer my mother's people of diabetes my parents traded
destinies my father died of diabetic complications   my mother of cancer
my maternal grandmother my aunt my father my youngest brother all
survived amputations their organs outlived their limbs i have always
wondered if i'd choose amputation

                                        if the question was amputate or die
what would i choose   but what if that isn't the choice i'm given what
if after all i'm claimed by the destiny of my father's people   what if

36

something else comes along my father's first stroke was at age forty-two
and at forty-seven and after my first trip in an ambulance they scanned
my brain to see if i'd had a stroke

                                        or what if my organs don't know how to
outlive my limbs what if my organs go first i worried for my heart and my
lungs and my brain after covid but they appear to be functional or at least
no one's said anything's wrong which is why i'm here writing lines for my
kidneys and drinking more water and eating dandelions

                                                maybe this isn't
how you write a poem for your kidneys but this is all i've got tonight

the blank canvas

friends have already asked
why there's a blank canvas
on the wall. they ask,
do i paint in secret?

no, i say, *i can't draw*
to save my life.
the blank canvas is there
because of my brother.

because he'd hang any
canvas he planned to
paint. never said why
he did it while it was blank.

and i wondered if
he wanted to plan
what he'd do and
how he'd go about it.

if he wanted to see how
the light or the shadows
moved across it during
the day or at night,

if he wanted to see
how it'd live with
all the other paintings
or with our meals,

with our conversations
with our mornings
with all our good days
and even the bad.

i'll hang a blank canvas
in every home i ever have
because i never want
to live terrified

of the blank space
the white page
i want to envision
what i'll do,

what i'll create
how it'll breathe
and how the light
will move across it.

what the curandera said

"se aprende por uno de dos caminos
el camino del amor o el camino del dolor"

(we learn by one of two roads,
the road of love or the road of pain)

i was made to survive catastrophe famine pain   broad shouldered and
able to go without sleep   i was too strong when i was young it made
me think i couldn't be broken   sleeping brought nightmares so i
learned to see in the dark   there was too much pain when i was young
so i learned not to cry not to whimper   sometimes we were hungry
there was too much work even when we were children   there was too
much madness when i was young   so i learned not to run from it
pulled my own madness out   and let it kill my eyes   let it terrify
others   it didn't terrify me until much later   because as a child it
saved me   kept me company

too much pain made me think nothing else was real   made me love
sharp edges and thorns and stubborn things that would die before
surrendering   too much pain made me think there was no other way to
live   only work and work and work and the body slowly breaking down
the mind always running running running so hard to rest when the work
wasn't done   i breathed in fear every second and felt it   crisis could
arrive at any minute   i could see it i knew it   more pain was
coming

i don't want any more of it   no more pain   no more learning from pain
greatest pain and greatest love collided   and i will never be myself
again without grief   so let me learn now only from the other road
i am filling myself with silence so that i can hear   i am filling myself
with sweetness so that i can see   i am filling myself with solitude so
that i can move gently and speak with peace   this also is a prayer

we say *rose*

and think the bloom think the
scent but the rose is also thorn
and stem and leaves and roots
and isn't everything that feeds
the rose also part of the rose
isn't the light that feeds the rose
and the rain that feeds the rose
a part of the rose they become

and isn't everything that touches
the rose also a part of the rose
the soil the roots nestle against
the air that carries the scent of rose
and when we touch the rose
isn't our skin even momentarily
a part of it and when we eat the rose
aren't we also the rose too

the sound of rain

i thought i imagined
the sound of rain last night

i walked out this morning
and all the ground was wet

puddles everywhere
all the trees' bark gone dark

cloudy skies overhead
and the soft scent of fallen rain

i should have known
i never imagine the sound of rain

it's either raining
or i'm calling the rain

what the hospice nurse asked

soon after they brought him home
and he was comfortable in the hospital bed
and the settings on the oxygen had been checked
and we had all the meds sorted and scheduled
and had gone through the list of needed supplies
and i'd made sure he wasn't thirsty or hungry
hot or cold in pain or nervous or too tired
the hospice nurse sat to ask us questions

she asked:
is there anything you need to say to each other?
is there anyone we're waiting for?
is there anything that needs to get done?
i traded a brief glance with him
and at the same time we both said
no. we're good.
and we were
we'd had five years since his amputation
to clear all the slates to forgive everything
to learn to be soft with each other
to recognize and to live as if life
was as precious as we always say it is
five years to plan for all possibilities
five years to know an end was coming
even if we didn't know if that end
was five or ten or twenty years away
and after all there was no one else to call
no one else he needed to see
and everything was done
everything he needed to do was done

the nurse looked startled
as if she hadn't expected
such a brief and clear answer
but she recovered and said
so, then, we're going to concentrate
on making you as comfortable as possible

i wondered how often her questions
sparked wails or debates or long lists
or confessions or rants or drawn out silences
if she had to referee and wrangle spouses
and children and parents and siblings and exes

after she left we rested
relieved to be home not at the hospital
no nurses or doctors or techs or janitors
coming by to check this or ask that or
give this or do that or take this
and he was surrounded by all his favorite
things his plants and his art and his laptop
and the pain meds were under my control
and we could order the days as we wished
however many days there were left

much later i thought
shouldn't we all live that way all the time
live knowing we have said everything
we need to say to everyone
that the ones we love know they are loved
and everything worked through that needed
to be worked through sometimes forgiven
sometimes condemned sometimes released
shouldn't we live without waiting for anyone
shouldn't we live having done what we most
needed to do or having done as much of it
as we could in the time that we had

the eaters of flowers

born soft born to unfurl
we could be gentle as flowers

hurting no one
making only beauty

we could be
entire languages of love

speaking tenderly
humming and illuminated

we could be
like the great beasts

tbat move across the
plains as if they were the skies

eaters of fruit and
eaters of seed and eaters of leaves

eaters of rain and
eaters of light and eaters of earth

but we are rarely gentle
rarely soft rarely tender rarely peaceful

that cannot be blamed solely
on our being devoted eaters of flesh

even as predators
we are eaters of flowers

we are eaters of time
eaters of memory eaters of beauty

eaters of what
was and what is to come

eaters of living
and eaters of dying

even as the living
and the dying devour us

is it possible to be truly gentle
before we have accepted we will die

and what is it to accept
that we are as delicate as the flowers

that our blooms are brief
that we are vulnerable to everything

too much not enough sun
too much not enough water

too much wind too
much touch too much pressure

that everything marks us
as if we too were petals with burnt edges

easier to dismiss the flowers
like we dismiss all the dead all the dying

easier to say each one isn't
precious after all they're everywhere

what would it mean to
pause each time we saw a flower and breathe

to take in the moment
that doesn't repeat and the light the scent

what would it mean to
think of each other as flowers

if every time we touched
we touched with fingers like petals

if every time we spoke
we spoke as if our mouths were flowers

our words a spill
of color our breath a spill of beauty

all my life i have been
thorn and root and wide strong stem

but it is time now for a different life
in the time that remains

to become an eater of flowers
to become flower

to pay attention as i never knew
how before

to watch how they drink in the sun
to watch the light in them

to listen to their gladness
in the morning sun

like them to turn my face
towards light and dew

to breathe without rushing to
bloom in the time i have

to accept to accept to accept
and one day fall

marigold

descanso

i notice them everywhere i go. i always have. today on the same street i saw three of them. different sizes. one not much more than a cross with plastic red and white roses. one covered in blue flowers and a wooden slat with a name and a date. and one with only slightly sun-faded star-and heart-shaped balloons. four bouquets of plastic flowers. mardi gras beads. a sunshine yellow cross with *blessed* written in turquoise paint.

when i see them i don't cross myself like i do when i pass by cemeteries and graveyard. i don't know what to call that fractional moment of acknowledgment which is me all at once crossing myself and sending a prayer and thinking of the deceased and thinking of the mourners and a small salutation to Death Herself. but all of that happens in a flash which is neither sad nor afraid but is real.

i think of how it makes sense to mark the place of loss with flowers and balloons and bright colors. how that sends a continuous burst of love to their lost one. how it must be a way to begin to heal the rip of sudden death. perhaps a painful death. and how acknowledging the loss hurts less than passing by that place and seeing nothing to mark where it happened.

what i have discovered in these months of loss is that the descanso for his loss is not necessarily where his body rests now. it's not even the place where he left this life. it doesn't matter where i am or where i go. i carry his descanso with me. everywhere i go. i carry it in my chest. here in my chest where his leaving left a hole so big there was hardly enough flesh to keep me together.

here in my chest is where i bring all the flowers. where i leave all the brightly ribboned memories. all the silver medallitas of all the things that meant so much to us both. where i carry all his favorite things. and where i put all the things he would have loved that he will never see or know or taste. here is where i will carry all the balloons lighter than air and heavier than grief.

i am the descanso.

the pain of the body is sacred

we talk about dignity
and we talk about choices

we talk about medication
and we talk about surgery

we talk about what is likely
and we talk about what isn't

we learn new phrases like
breakthrough pain

we learn to count hours
between permitted doses

i see things i hadn't seen
before—red flesh, white bone

i see pain beyond all bearing
and wonder that it can be survived

what i learned all those years ago
was that the pain of the body is sacred

it is a sacred thing to witness this
to hold all of this in my heart

how the body is wounded
how the body falters
how the body heals
how the body weeps
how the body breaks
how the body is a ruin

how we cared for the body of the one we loved
how we poured love into the body of the one we loved
how even at the end it was hard to remove our hands
to let go of their hands to not touch their face
to not think *i didn't know it would be so soon*

we didn't know
that all of it was sacred

my mother would say

mis muertitos
'my dead'
in the diminutive

claiming all her dead with
unfaded undimmed unending
love and affection

i say when anyone
will listen that she taught me
how to mourn

as if she knew she
would leave me when i was young
as if she knew i would have much to mourn

or perhaps it was because
i was the first child born
after her mother died

i don't know the dates
sometimes i wonder if i floated
in tears and not amniotic fluid

she taught me by
remembering and remembering
her own mother

what her mother loved
how her mother spoke
what her mother believed

and i knew how to mourn
my own mother how it was less
pain and more love to remember

to speak all the time of what
she loved and what she said and
what she taught me

my mother knew no distant
way to think of her ancestors
or her beloved dead

i think she would have had
compassion for those who are
awkward in the face of grief

awkward because
grief hasn't yet visited them
or because they weren't taught

and they don't know
or cannot accept that death
is not the opposite of life

only the next part
the next world
the doorway we'll all enter

no one taught me
to fear death and i never
learned it on my own

i wonder now
because i spend days
all my days in contemplation

if this is a form of meditation
this remembering the dead
who are gone

but also not gone
to mourn and mourn deeply
in all directions in time

i cannot make new memories
with mis muertitos
but it crosses my mind all the time

they would have loved this
this would have made them laugh
and this would have made them weep

as fiercely as i might laugh or live
what do i call this
new way of walking

this sense that
every other step is in the
next world not this one

it isn't that they are with me
it's that part of me
is already with them

alone

these are
narrow
and
precarious
roads
and
sometimes
not even
loved ones
can walk
with
you

i am
beginning
to respect
it
this
solitude
needed
for
remembering
and
listening

how
do we
fashion
our
lives
after loss
only
a few of
the grieving
understand

so many
choose

to distract
themselves
to return
they say
return
to something
others
can call
normal

for some
of us
grief
requires
space
great great
amounts
of space
and hours
of alone

the other
day
i said
the word
recalibrate
i think
i meant it
because
suddenly
being
just myself
is an
infinite
thing

it's been 6 months

h o w can this be...   ...it's only been 5 m i n u t e
s...   ...or maybe it's been 5 y e a r s...   ...since
the last time i said g o o d b y e...   ...since the last time
i t o u c h e d his face...   ...6 months of feeling like a
displaced and d e s t r i n g e d marionette   learning how
to b r e a t h e and e a t and s l e e p on her own...   ...i've
never b e f o r e lived with this kind of s i l e n c e...   ...it
e x t e n d s on and on and on...   ...i don't think my b o d y
is the s a m e body i had half a year ago...   ...that body was
afraid and anxious and n e v e r slept...   ...this body has s u r
v i v e d something else it didn't know it could survive...   ...
this body will n e v e r hear that voice...   ...this body had to
b u i l d itself until it was s t r o n g enough to weep...   ...
this body is made up of more t e a r s is more salt soaked than
that body ever was...   ...leaving me bestowing s t r a n g
e l y worded blessings...   ...may you r e m a i n innocent
of this kind of loss...   ...may you n e v e r feel a
hurt this deep...

my brother was born on the day of the dead
my mother who didn't know how to be afraid of death
saw it i think as an auspicious omen because he almost didn't
survive to be born because my father hadn't wanted him to be born
afraid that something would be wrong with him as if we hadn't all
been born more than a little wrong into a world that didn't
try all that hard to make us less wrong less hurt

my brother wrote a poem about our great great maybe it
was only one great grandmother who lived to be 115 years old
who was exiled by her family to a shack who lived like an animal
my father said because she was a full blooded india and the family
was ashamed and maybe they thought if she lived outside she
wouldn't teach any of her descendants to be indios like she was
as if they could will away what she was what they were

my brother wrote that she must have cursed us all
of her descendants living and to come with the same darkness
that made our great great maybe only one great grandfather decide
to set a time and date and then announce his death to his entire
family to order and pay for the food and pan dulce for the
reception and then i presume to dress himself and shine his boots
and select the rope and hang himself at 4 in the afternoon

my brother survived his time in the womb survived and grew to be
the tallest and strongest of us all survived and was born without
causing any pain to our mother was born humming and content and
perhaps already dreaming of flowers and earth and delicious food
and music and words and all the things he was born already loving
but i think it gave my heart a little pause a strange little echo told me it
was important that he was born on the day of the dead

i had to travel 2000 miles northward to learn about altars and the
day of the dead built my first altar in upstate new york and later
tied what i learned there to my mother's memories of graveyards in
south texas it was in new york that i learned the significance of
marigolds to the day of the dead i don't have my mother's or my
brother's talent or passion for growing gardens but i think that was
when i started the garden of marigolds in my heart

and time and life converted those gardens into entire fields so vast
you could walk from sunup to sundown and never see the
beginning or end of them and i wrote a story about a girl named
cempasuchil and i tasted marigold petals and ate their color and
their velvet feel and their histories of sunlight and people say they
have a favorite flower but i don't think that's true i think
sometimes a flower might decide to claim us to name us their own

my mother didn't tell me or maybe she didn't know to tell me as
she only lived to be 13 years older than i am now that i would need
all those fields of marigolds because now that my brother is gone
every day is his borning day and every day is his dying day and
every day is the day of the dead and this means i have a
tremendous need for infinite marigolds

what my brother said

it was during his last stay in the hospital we were talking or eating or
streaming a show on his laptop or napping or staring out the window or
any of those dozen things people do when time doesn't make sense
anymore and days and nights and hours blur and mostly the time is spent
keeping each other company and listening to each other breathe and i was
very comfortable because they'd brought me a spare hospital bed when it
was obvious that i had no plans to leave that i would remain for every last
minute he had and they even made a notation in his file that i could
request guest meal trays so that i wouldn't even have to leave to find food
and i could see that things were different when the patient was in end of
life care not like 5 years before after the amputation when i slept in chairs
or on the hard floor for two months and haunted the hospital cafeteria two
or three times a day until the cashiers took pity on me and gave me
the senior discount at every meal even though i was more than a dozen years
too young

but it was during this last stay that he suddenly paused and i could feel the
loud energy of the sudden silence and then he said in his poet voice a
voice i hadn't heard in years the voice he used to read his poetry with the
voice that was soft spoken and gentle but that had rendered entire
roomfuls of people quiet and motionless he said

> you woke up covered in leaves
> and honey
> and the flowers of the day

and i knew in that moment that those words were important and that it was
beautiful and i wrote them down and i even thought oh we'll never have
that shared tattoo we swore we'd get and i thought maybe i should tattoo
these words on my skin and keep them close and remember this moment
and the light in the hospital room and the clarity and power of his voice
and these days and that those words might be the last lines of poetry he'd
ever compose and what a beautiful image what a beautiful gift those words
are

and then we went home where he lived his last days and he and i lived his
last days and time warped this way and that and then he was gone and then
i was almost gone too and then there was the business of learning to live

on my own and the business of possessions and overhauling our home till
it became my home and so many doctors' visits and new medications and
listening to the silence and the work of solitary solitary solitary living and
at some point enough of my mind returned that i went back to writing to
putting words on the page to figuring out how to tell the story of where i was

for two months i looked through everything through sticky notes and
journals and calendars through my phone and my messages and
documents on my laptop and texts and emails and every spare piece of
paper and i spent nights combing through memories and attempting to
recall where i'd been and what i'd thought and why why why hadn't i
been more careful because i couldn't find anywhere the words he'd said
and i couldn't remember them precisely and they were nowhere to be
found and i thought about how even when we try our memories are not
infallible and how we don't remember things the way they happened

and i was afraid i'd have to write a poem about the lines i lost and how
everything everything everything was subject to loss and that all i'd
retained was *flowers of the day* and that the fragment would break me
every day of my life for having lost something i knew was precious when i
first heard it that i knew was precious enough to shelter forever and i
thought i'd have to write a poem about this forgotten thing and how we
forget everything and how it is impossible to reclaim what is lost

but tonight while looking for something else i found his words and it was a
blooming in my heart for all that is lost has been lost will be lost at least i
know these words aren't these words have returned to me these words will
stay with me forever and now here they are written down so that i'll
always be able to find them and they'll keep me company and sit with me
through hours that may stretch into strange infinities or vanish in a blink
they'll stay with me for as long as i can read or for as long as i can listen
to someone else speak them oh someone bury these words with me so that
i never lose them

gracias a mis diosas

all my prayers were answered
he didn't die afraid
he didn't die in pain
he didn't die alone

and what i prayed for
most fervently
for years and years
every time i left our home
every time i went to work
every time i went to sleep
was that he would die
before i did
because i didn't want him
to have to endure a day without me
defenseless
in the world

my prayers were granted
it might be that i don't
pray for anything anymore
Creator told me that
there is only one mandate now
to create
and i've set myself the tasks
of making myself stronger
so that i can do as much work
as i can in the time i have left
of loving everyone i love
and will love
of holding all my remaining moments
as precious and beautiful
of saying thank you thank you
thank you with my
every remaining
breath

the last poem

about the last poem

In June of 2022, I was commissioned by Texas Highways Magazine to write a poem responding to the tragic events at Robb Elementary School in Uvalde, TX on May 24, 2022. A school shooting left 19 students and 2 teachers dead and many more injured.

For twenty years, I'd read my brother all my first drafts. He'd weigh every sound, every image, every thought. Two weeks before my brother's last trip to a hospital, I read him my first draft of this poem. And even at that point, he offered essential feedback.

This is the last poem I read him. The last poem he helped me with.

after the Robb Elementary School shooting,
May 24, 2022

my eyes are not large enough to weep this grief
my arms are not wide enough to hold this grief
my tongue is not wise enough to soothe this grief
my heart my sometimes infinite heart is not enough
this time

i don't know where mothers hold their grief
or fathers or children or friends or neighbors or even
strangers who in this shared hurt are no longer strangers
our chests are not large enough can't hold this roiling of
heat of fire of confusion this churning of fear of rawness
of emptiness

are tears enough are flowers enough are songs enough
are gifts enough are condolences enough are prayers enough
none of us are strong enough to bear this alone
one grief touches another one hurt touches another
one loss touches another one absence touches another
always linking

we bring what we can hold what we can we weep with you
may all our tears lessen the weight of your grief
may you never feel alone never feel abandoned in grief
never feel that we have forgotten that they are forgotten
they are loved
they are loved
they are loved

Acknowledgments

With thanks to these publications for publishing current or earlier versions of the following poems:

"for Uvalde" in *Texas Highways Magazine*

"descanso," "the pain of the body is sacred," and "my mother would say" in *Tikkun*

"cempasuchil" in *A Gathering Of Tribes*

"the sounds of rain" and "the eaters of flowers" in *Huizache*

"puño de flores" in *The Austin Chronicle*

"we say rose" in *Sierra Magazine*

"poem for my kidneys" and "what the curandera said" in *Oyedrum*

"in my heart," "it's the old hunger to grow wild," and "Lot K32" at poemoftheweek.com

"the story of my four hearts" and "i know they mean well when they say my brother is still with me" in *Acentos Review*

About ire'ne lara silva

ire'ne lara silva, the 2023 Texas State Poet Laureate, is the author of four poetry collections, *furia*, *Blood Sugar Canto*, *CUICACALLI/House of Song*, and *FirstPoems*, two chapbooks, *Enduring Azucares* and *Hibiscus Tacos*, and a short story collection, *flesh to bone*, which won the Premio Aztlán.

ire'ne is the recipient of a 2021 Tasajillo Writers Grant, a 2017 NALAC Fund for the Arts Grant, the final Alfredo Cisneros del Moral Award,

and was the Fiction Finalist for AROHO's 2013 Gift of Freedom Award.

Most recently, ire'ne was awarded the 2021 Texas Institute of Letters Shrake Award for Best Short Nonfiction.

ire'ne is currently a Writer at Large for Texas Highways Magazine and is working on a second collection of short stories titled, *the light of your body*.

Find her at irenelarasilva.wordpress.com